Although the United
trative power creates
government. The res
administrative state v.   States. The state within is sometimes called the "regulatory state" to emphasize its burdens on economic and per-
sonal freedom, and is sometimes called the "deep state"
because of its tendency to interfere with our elected government. This book focuses on the legal side of the problem – on the power claimed by the administrative state
and how it slices through basic civil liberties.

Not Just Economics

Over the past century, most complaints about administrative power have come from an economic perspective. It is
said that administrative power is inefficient, dangerously
centralized, burdensome on business, destructive of jobs,
and stifling for innovation and growth. All of this is pain-
fully true, but these are largely economic complaints, and
economic complaints are not the entire critique of administrative power.

Although this power began as an exceptional method
of regulation, and was applied mostly to corporations, it
has become the dominant reality of American governance,

which intrudes into the full range of American life, including not only economic endeavors but also political participation and personal decisions.

The economic critique does not address the breadth of this danger. Indeed, it tends to protest merely the degree of administrative regulation, and it thereby usually accepts the legitimacy of administrative power – as long as it is not too heavy-handed on business. No wonder the economic criticism has not stopped the growth of administrative power.

The Centrality of the Legal Challenge

For a better understanding of the administrative threat, one must turn to law. The legal critique more fully addresses the problem than does the economic protest, for although much administrative power is economically inefficient, all of it is unconstitutional. And this legal objection is central, because it confronts administrative power on its own terms – on its pretension to bind Americans in the manner of law.

In saying that administrative power is unconstitutional, this is not to deny that executive power is extensive. Executive power is often portrayed as merely the power to execute the laws, but more accurately (as recognized by Alexander Hamilton) it amounts to the power to execute all of the nation's lawful force. It thus includes the power to prosecute offenders in court, to exercise discretion in distributing benefits, to determine the status of immigrants, and so forth.

In contrast, administrative power involves not force but legal obligation, and this is why the legal challenge matters so much. Contemporary theorists sometimes suggest that law is a sovereign's command backed by coercion. But traditionally in America, notably when the Constitution was adopted, law was something that came with legal obligation – the obligation to obey. Working from underlying ideas about consent, eighteenth-century Americans assumed that a rule could have the obligation of law only if it came from the constitutionally established legislature elected by the people, and that a judicial decision could have such obligation only if it came from a constitutionally appointed judge exercising independent judgment. On the basis of such principles, the US Constitution placed lawmaking power in Congress and judicial power in the courts. The power to bind – that is, to create legal obligation – was thus in these departments, not the executive.

Nonetheless, through administrative power, the executive purports to create legal obligation. It binds Americans and deprives them of their liberty, not through acts of Congress and acts of the courts but through other mechanisms.

And this evasion of the Constitution's pathways for law is what makes the legal objection to administrative power so central.

Adding to the problem, administrative power also evades many of the Constitution's procedures, including both its legislative and judicial processes. Administrative power thereby sidesteps most of the Constitution's procedural freedoms.

Administrative power is thus all about the evasion of governance through law, including an evasion of constitutional processes and procedural rights. These legal problems are forceful reasons to reject all administrative power and, indeed, to consider it the civil liberties issue of our time.

Absolute Power, Then and Now

An initial step toward understanding the danger and unconstitutionality of administrative power is to examine some examples, past and present. Although our republic may seem too American and contemporary to bear comparison with England's old absolute monarchy, the similarities are therefore all the more disturbing.

English absolutism was epitomized by King James I, who ruled from 1603 to 1625. Rather than being content with the government's regular power to make statutes in

Parliament and to have cases adjudicated in the courts, he tried to exercise versions of legislative and judicial powers in his "prerogative" commissions or tribunals – his equivalent of administrative agencies. And his capacity in these bodies to bind his subjects was a significant part of what was called his "absolute power."

His prerogative tribunals most famously included the Star Chamber and the High Commission. The one had statutory authorization for some of its jurisdiction, and the other was entirely founded on statute. With or without legislative authorization, these bodies exercised absolute power.

Such tribunals are often assumed to have been blood-soaked torture chambers, but they were more bureaucratic than bloody. They were efficient prerogative agencies, and they exercised absolute power in ways that have come back to life in America.

LAWMAKING. Instead of legislating through acts of Parliament, King James personally issued proclamations in the Star Chamber that served as binding regulations on trade, manufacturing, and urban development. He even had these proclamations published in a volume that looked like a statute book – an early equivalent of the *Federal Register*.

James undoubtedly had the power to issue proclamations, but proclamations that bound in the manner of law were another matter. In 1610, after James used proclamations to create regulatory offenses, Chief Justice Edward Coke and the other chief judges declared such proclamations unlawful and void, saying that the king "by his proclamation cannot create any offense which was not an offense before." The judges recognized that lawmaking outside of the legislature was unlawful.

Ever tempted to exert more power with less effort, rulers are rarely content to govern merely through the law, and in their restless desire to escape its pathways, many of them try to work through other mechanisms. These other modes of binding subjects are absolute power.

James, however, had other means of legislating outside of Parliament – most notably, Star Chamber regulations, which were issued more bureaucratically than his personal proclamations. Acting through its adjudicatory proceedings, the Star Chamber could issue regulations in the form of judicial decrees. In other words, judicial-style process was used for lawmaking, and this practice came to an end only when Parliament in 1641 abolished the Star Chamber.

In the twentieth century, the sort of power exercised by King James was revived in the United States. With remarkable fidelity to the old absolutism, some federal agencies used adjudicatory-style proceedings as a basis for issuing binding rules – a process known as "formal rule making." Because such proceedings came to seem cumbersome, agencies nowadays issue binding rules with little-more ceremony than giving notice and soliciting public comments – this being called "informal rule making." Either way, like their seventeenth-century precursors, federal agencies are engaged in lawmaking.

The Affordable Care Act, for example, authorizes Health and Human Services to issue binding rules on health care. Indeed, many federal agencies make binding rules with express authorization. This sort of administrative rule making is justified on the fiction that when Congress states an "intelligible principle," agencies that follow the principle are merely specifying what Congress has enacted. But this is a fantasy. The crude reality, as recognized long ago by James Landis (a prominent advocate of administrative power) is that the agencies are exercising legislative power.

INTERPRETATION. Not content with overt prerogative lawmaking, James also used his prerogative tribunals to make law through what he called the "interpretation" of statutes. Where statutes seemed ambiguous or indefinite, the Star Chamber and the High Commission used interpretation to

make law. And to ensure that these prerogative interpretations had legal effect, James demanded judicial deference
to them.

The judges, however, stood their ground; they generally refused to defer. As Chief Justice Coke explained to
James in 1610, although the king appointed judges, he
lacked judicial office. In contrast, the judges had the office
of judging and interpreting. The judges therefore could not
defer to the king's interpretations.

Of course, what really was at stake was not James's
personal interpretations of statutes but the interpretations
put forth by his prerogative tribunals. Correspondingly,
Coke's point was that although the members of these bodies acted as the king's agents, even the king himself could
not make authoritative interpretations of law.

The king and his minions obviously had to interpret
statutes every day to decide the lawfulness of their own
conduct – just as any individual regularly had to interpret
statutes to avoid violating the law. And in making such
decisions, all such persons could rely on the judgment of
their lawyers. But authoritative interpretations came only
from the judges, for only they had an office of independent
judgment in deciding cases. Because of their office or duty
to exercise independent judgment, and because the king's
interpretations were without such authority, the judges

could not defer to the interpretations that came from the king's agents or agencies.

The lawmaking interpretation that James desired for his prerogative bodies has become a reality for American administrative agencies. Federal judges show varying degrees of deference to agency interpretations, and the agencies therefore can use their interpretations to create law.

Most famously, under the 1984 Supreme Court case *Chevron v. National Resources Defense Council*, judges must defer to administrative interpretations of ambiguities in statutes. Such interpretations must be among the "permissible" possible interpretations, but within this standard, agencies generally enjoy much freedom to choose their interpretations and thus to make law wherever they can find a plausible statutory ambiguity. As a result, even where Congress has not expressly authorized administrative rule making, agencies often can use interpretation to make binding rules – that is, to make law.

This can be illustrated by the Clean Power Plan – an Environmental Protection Agency (EPA) rule designed to reduce greenhouse gas emissions by establishing emission standards for existing power plants. Most commentators protest its substance (for example, its destruction of jobs), but the point here is how the agency made the rule. According to the EPA, it can issue the rule because it is merely interpreting an ambiguous section of the Clean Air Act (§111d). Similarly, the EPA relies on interpretation to make its rule on the waters of the United States – a rule that potentially regulates almost all waters in the nation (admittedly not puddles, but nearly everything else).

Even where an agency does not interpret a statute with the formality required for *Chevron* deference, it can issue less formal statutory interpretation. Although such interpretation does not get as much deference from the courts as the formally issued sort, it receives what the courts call "respect" under the so-called *Mead-Skidmore* doctrine, and this is enough for agencies to use informal interpretation as a means of legislating.

Topping it off, agencies make law not only by interpreting statutes but also by interpreting their own rules, often in the form of guidance. And this sort of interpretation gets great judicial deference under *Auer v. Robbins*. An agency can thus both issue a binding rule and interpret it, and at each stage it is making law.

These methods of lawmaking through agency interpretation are disturbing. They are pathways for agencies to do what Congress itself did not do, or even expressly authorize. And they revive a mode of lawmaking that once flourished under James I.

ADJUDICATION AND PROCEDURAL RIGHTS. In addition to using the Star Chamber and High Commission for lawmaking, King James also used them for adjudication. These prerogative tribunals employed civilian-style inquisitorial proceedings. Accordingly, in relying on these tribunals, James escaped not only the courts and their judges but also their juries and the full range of their procedural rights.

Medieval kings had already tried to evade the courts and their processes by summoning, trying, and punishing subjects in prerogative proceedings. In response, fourteenth-century statutes confined kings to acting through the "due process of law." As put by a medieval summary of the most comprehensive of these statutes, "None shall be put to answer without due process of law." Sixteenth- and seventeenth-century kings, however, used the Star Chamber and High Commission to bind subjects, and King James and his son Charles I took this so far as to provoke profound opposition. Many lawyers complained that prerogative adjudication violated the due process of law, and their protests concluded in 1641 with the abolition of both the Star Chamber and the High Commission.

Like the old prerogative courts, contemporary administrative tribunals evade the courts, their judges, their juries, and the due process of law. Administrative tribunals sometimes apply inquisitorial methods, but even where their proceedings are adversarial, they do not live up to the Constitution's procedural guarantees. The Securities Exchange Commission (SEC), for example, can bring civil insider-trading cases in federal courts, or it can refer insider-trading cases to the Justice Department for it to prosecute criminally in such courts, and either way, defendants get judges and juries and the full range of the Constitution's applicable procedural rights. But the SEC can also pursue insider-trading cases before administrative law judges, who work for the commission, are not really judges, do not offer juries, and do not even allow equal discovery.

Like their prerogative predecessors, moreover, administrative adjudicators cannot question the lawfulness of the regulations they enforce. It often is said that administrative law judges are independent because they are protected in their tenure and salary. But actually they can be demoted or have their salary docked if they reject administrative regulations as unlawful. This is especially problematic because an underlying question in all administrative proceedings concerns the unlawfulness of the applicable regulations, not least under the Constitution. It thus becomes apparent that administrative law judges are precommitted to upholding the government's position on the most persistent and serious legal questions. And this means that they usually are systematically biased in favor of one of the parties before them, in violation of the due process of law. Once again, administrative adjudication echoes the past.

WAIVERS. Finally, James I and most other sixteenth- and seventeenth-century English kings claimed a power to suspend the law or at least dispense with it. The suspending power allowed the king to suspend a statute's obligation for all persons; the dispensing power enabled him to dispense with its obligation for particular named persons. In both ways, a king could evade the need to persuade Parliament to repeal or amend a statute and, instead, could simply relieve some or all subjects of their duty to comply.

This waiver power was widely criticized. It was open to corruption and political favoritism, and it left subjects unequal under the law and in the courts. Eventually, in 1689, the English Declaration of Rights declared the suspending and dispensing powers unlawful unless exercised with Parliamentary consent. And in the next century, at least some Englishmen considered any use of these powers incompatible with the division of executive and legislative power between the Crown and Parliament. As to the suspending power, for example, it was said that "the constitution has entrusted the crown with no power to suspend any act of Parliament, under any circumstances whatever." In other words, royal or executive power could never include the power to unmake law.

Nowadays, the prerogative to suspend and dispense with the law has been revived in administrative waivers. The waivers sometimes are authorized by statute and sometimes are not – as with the so-called mini-med waivers issued under the Affordable Care Act. Either way, waivers are agency letters that tell persons they are excused from complying with a statute or a regulation under it, thus placing them above the law. Although usually issued, like the old dispensations, to particular persons, waivers can be given to all affected parties, so as to create the effect of the old suspending power.

*   *   *

In one instance after another, contemporary administrative power echoes the old absolutism. In place of prerogative lawmaking, we have administrative lawmaking. Instead of prerogative adjudication, we have administrative adjudication. Rather than the prerogative evasion of procedural rights, we have the administrative evasion of such rights. And instead of royal dispensations and suspensions, we have administrative waivers.

The old absolutism thus seems to have crawled out

the grave and come back to life. Of course, the contemporary version is only "soft absolutism," exercised not for a monarch but for the masses. Nonetheless, as Alexis de Tocqueville recognized, this is more than dangerous enough.

What Is Absolute Power?

In exactly what sense does administrative power revive absolute power? Put more broadly, what could explain the remarkable parallels between the old and the contemporary – between the prerogative and the administrative?

The answer rests ultimately on human nature. Ever tempted to exert more power with less effort, rulers are rarely content to govern merely through the law, and in their restless desire to escape its pathways, many of them try to work through other mechanisms. These other modes of binding subjects are absolute power, and once one understands this, it is not altogether surprising that absolute power is a recurring problem and that American administrative power revives it.

Some commentators in the first half of the twentieth century denounced administrative power as "absolute" without really understanding what absolutism was. They used the word loosely to condemn discretion and anything they did not like. But the term "absolute power"

Administrative power is a preconstitutional mode of governance – the very sort of power that constitutions were most clearly expected to prevent.

traditionally had very specific meanings, one of which is especially important for understanding administrative power – namely, that absolute power is extralegal power. From this perspective, absolute power includes all efforts to bind (or impose legal obligation) not merely through law and the courts but through other pathways.

Put more instrumentally, absolute power can be understood as an evasion of law. It has been a means by which rulers, whether in a monarchy or a republic, avoid the trouble of binding persons merely through acts of the legislature and of the courts, and instead impose legal obligation through other sorts of edicts. In this sense, absolute power is an evasion of the regular paths of governance, and this is why it has been a repeated problem across the centuries.

The evasion, moreover, is why administrative power has continually expanded. There has been (as Gary Lawson observes) a continual "rise and rise" of the administrative state, and this is no coincidence. Being not law but a mode of evasion, which flows around law and law-like things, administrative power has flowed around the Constitution's pathways of power and even around formal administrative pathways, thus creating a cascade of evasions.

Of course, extralegal power has sometimes been expressly authorized by statute, and sometimes not (as evident nowadays from most administrative interpretations and some waivers). But with or without statutory authorization, when government imposes legal obligation through acts other than those of the legislature and the courts, it is not acting merely through the law. Its power is therefore extralegal and, in this sense, absolute.

Incidentally, although absolute power was most centrally understood as extralegal power, the phrase "absolute power" had other possible meanings, one of them being unlimited power. English kings thus had some "absolute" powers that did not bind or unbind their subjects, but were considered absolute in the sense that they were entirely, and thus without limitation, in the hands of the monarch — indeed, inherent in him. For example, he alone could pardon offenders and enter agreements with foreign rulers. But such powers did not purport to create or displace legal obligation and were soon brought under law, and they therefore were considered lawful and unproblematic elements of royal or executive power. Indeed, the US Constitution treats pardons and foreign agreements as part of the president's lawful executive power. Tellingly, however, if a foreign agreement is to be binding as domestic law, the president must get the Senate to ratify it as a treaty.

Power thus can be considered absolute for different reasons, but the absolutism that matters here is extralegal power – the power that binds not merely through acts of the legislature or the courts but through other sorts of edicts. This was the key problem with much of the king's old prerogative power, and it remains the central problem with contemporary American administrative power. Put another way, under the US Constitution, legislative and judicial acts are the only ways for the federal government, at the national level, to create domestic legal obligation. Accordingly, when the government binds persons through other paths, its acts are extralegal and, in this sense, absolute.

The extralegal or absolute character of administrative power is very revealing. At the very least, it shows that absolute power is a recurring danger. In addition, as now will be seen, it allows one to understand that constitutional law developed in response to this threat.

The Constitutional Rejection of Absolute Power

In justifying federal administrative power as constitutional, its apologists often suggest that administrative power is a modern development, which therefore could not have been anticipated by the US Constitution. Early Americans, however, were familiar with English constitutional history, and they therefore were well aware of the danger from absolute power and its extralegal paths.

The English in the seventeenth century largely repudiated the absolute powers with which monarchs bound their subjects extralegally. James I seriously abused absolute power, but it was left to his son Charles I to take it to the limit and thereby provoke open resistance and eventually a civil war. In 1641, just before the conflict, Parliament abolished the two primary prerogative tribunals, the Star Chamber and the High Commission, which carried out most of the king's extralegal lawmaking, interpretation, and adjudication. Later, one of Charles I's sons, James II, would live up to his namesake's failings and thereby prompt the English Revolution of 1688; and one result was that Parliament the next year, in the Declaration of Rights, began what would become a repudiation of the suspending and dispensing powers.

Underlying these events were English constitutional ideas. The very notion of constitutional law developed in England to defeat the extralegal aspects of absolutism, and constitutional law was therefore inextricably intertwined with the question of absolute power. Some notable English lawyers expounded the ideal that kings had to rule through acts of Parliament and the courts, not through other edicts. Some added that, under the English constitution, legislative power was in Parliament, judicial power in the judges, and executive power in the Crown. On this understanding, the English constitution left no room for the Crown to bind subjects extralegally. Of course, the English constitution was merely unwritten custom, and it thus was open to multiple and often conflicting ideals. But the English constitutional vision that rejected absolutism and its extralegal power would appeal to Americans.

Early Americans tended to understand that constitutional law had developed in England as a means of barring absolute power. They therefore were determined in their constitutions to be even more systematic than the English in precluding a revival of the absolute prerogative or anything like it.

Just how much Americans viewed such power with horror is apparent from John Adams. In 1776, he observed that his countrymen aimed to establish governments in which a governor or president had "the whole executive power, after divesting it of those badges of domination called prerogatives" – by which Adams meant, of course, the absolute prerogatives. Similarly, when James Madison in *Federalist* 48 worried about legislative tyranny, he noted that the "founders of our republics ... never for a moment ...

turned their eyes from the danger to liberty from the over-
grown and all-grasping prerogative of an hereditary magistrate." Indeed, he worried that Americans went so far in
worrying about the prerogative that they were paying
insufficient attention the danger from the legislature.

Americans thus were fully aware of the threat from
absolute power and its extralegal paths, and they feared
that this dangerous mode of governance might come back
to life. To be sure, the term "administrative power" was
not yet ordinarily used in England or America. But absolute
power was a familiar problem and much on the minds of
Americans. It therefore should be no surprise that, in the
US Constitution, they adopted structures and rights that
systematically barred this danger.

The Constitution's Structures

How exactly does the US Constitution bar administrative
power? Most basically, the Constitution's broad structures
systematically preclude extralegal or absolute power. The
revival of such power, whether called "prerogative" or
"administrative," is therefore unconstitutional.

Incidentally, the argument here about the unconstitutionality of administrative power (whether in this section
on structure or the next section on rights) relies on the

Constitution's early history and may therefore prompt anxieties about originalism and attempts to return to the past. Such concerns, however, have little application here, for administrative power has already returned America to the past – not to the constitutionalism of 1789 but to something more like the absolutism of about 1610. Although administrative power is a softer absolutism than that of James I, it nonetheless is a preconstitutional mode of governance – the very sort of power that constitutions were most clearly expected to prevent. A great lurch backward has thus already occurred, and the underlying constitutional questions are not about refinements of interpretation but about things as basic as whether Americans will be governed solely through law and whether they will enjoy the Constitution's procedural rights.

ARTICLES I AND III. The Constitution establishes only regular avenues of power, and thereby blocks irregular or extralegal power. To be precise, it blocks extralegal lawmaking by placing legislative power exclusively in Congress, and it prevents extralegal adjudication by placing judicial power exclusively in the courts.

It thus authorizes only two pathways for government to bind Americans, in the sense of imposing legal obligation on them. Although a few exceptions will be noted later, the government generally can impose binding rules only through acts of Congress (or treaties ratified by the Senate), and can impose binding adjudications only through acts of the courts. These are its lawful options. Other attempts to bind Americans, whether with rules or adjudications, are unconstitutional.

Rather than merely arcana of government structure, these are core civil liberties issues. Binding agency rules deny Americans their right under Article I to be subject to only such federal legislation as is enacted by an elected Congress, and such rules thereby dilute the constitutional right to vote. Moreover, binding agency adjudications deprive Americans of their right under Article III to be subject only to such federal judicial decisions as come from a court, with a real judge, a jury, and the full due process of law. Thus, even before one gets to the violations of enumerated constitutional rights, it should be apparent that the administrative evasions of the Constitution's pathways for binding power come with severe consequences for constitutional freedom.

DELEGATION. Administrative lawmaking is often justified as delegated power – as if Congress could divest itself of the power that the people had delegated to it. The Constitution, however, expressly bars any such subdelegation.

This conclusion may initially seem odd, for the Constitution contains no nondelegation clause. How, then, does the Constitution bar congressional subdelegation? The answer comes in the Constitution's first substantive word. The document begins: "All legislative powers herein granted shall be vested in a Congress . . ." If all legislative powers are to be in Congress, they cannot be elsewhere. If the grant were merely permissive, not exclusive, there would be no reason for the word *All*. That word bars subdelegation.

When it came to the judicial power, the Constitution in Article III established only the Supreme Court and left Congress free to establish other courts. The Constitution therefore could not say that "all judicial power" shall be vested in any particular court or courts. All the same, Article III does not allow the judges to subdelegate their power, for it was well understood at the time that judicial power, by its nature, could not be delegated. As it happens, the civil law, drawing on Roman law, allowed judges to subdelegate their judicial power. But the common-law vision of a judge precluded any such subdelegation. For example, although judges could rely on clerks and special masters for many purposes, they could not rely on them to exercise judgment in a case.

The Constitution's barriers to any subdelegation of legislative or judicial power may sound merely technical, but they were expressions of an old and crucial principle against subdelegation, which underlay the efficacy of constitutions. The logic was that once the people had delegated different powers to the different branches of government, any subdelegation of such powers would allow the government to evade the structure of government chosen by the people. Alas, this has happened.

Significantly, however, the Supreme Court has not openly embraced delegation. At least when discussing expressly authorized rule making, the Court claims that binding agency rules are not delegated lawmaking but rather are merely specifications of the law – this being the theory of how agencies give effect to congressional expressions of "intelligible principles." Although this theory is a mere fig leaf, which does not really cover agencies' naked exercise of subdelegated legislative power, it is revealing that the Supreme Court remains committed to the idea that administrative lawmaking does not involve delegated lawmaking. Although the Court is deluding no one but itself, it thereby makes clear its understanding that the Constitution bars any subdelegation.

WAIVERS. Not only in making law but also in unmaking it through waivers, administrative power is unconstitutional. And courts cannot constitutionally give waivers any effect.

When the Constitution places all legislative powers in Congress, it gives Congress not only the power to make law but also the power to unmake it. And it thereby bars the executive from suspending or dispensing with the law. When the Constitution, moreover, places the judicial power in the courts and guarantees the due process of law, it precludes the executive from telling the courts not to apply the law, and prevents the courts from abandoning their own judgment about what the law requires.

Note that some state constitutions carefully preserved a limited executive suspending power, and the US Constitution authorized a legislative suspension of habeas corpus in narrow circumstances. It thus becomes all the more apparent that the Constitution generally does not permit administrative waivers. Nonetheless, waivers are now commonplace.

Although waivers reduce regulatory burdens for the well connected, they increase the burdens for others. Anticipating the availability of waivers, the government often feels free to impose overly constraining rules. As a result, those who do not get waivers usually suffer under especially restrictive regulations.

NECESSARY AND PROPER. The Necessary and Proper Clause authorizes Congress to make all laws that are "necessary and proper" for carrying out the government's other powers, and the clause is therefore usually said to allow Congress to create administrative power. But the clause needs to be read more carefully.

The usual argument from the Necessary and Proper Clause takes for granted that Congress is authorized to do what is necessary and proper for carrying out the government's powers in the abstract. From this perspective, Congress can give effect to the legislative and judicial powers by shifting them partly to administrative agencies.

But the Necessary and Proper Clause actually gives Congress only the power to carry out the government's other powers as they are "vested" by the Constitution in various departments and persons. This focus on vested powers precludes Congress from using the clause to rearrange or otherwise unvest any such powers. Of particular significance here, the clause does not allow Congress to shift the powers vested in Congress or the courts to administrative agencies.

And even if one were to imagine that the Necessary and

Guarantees of due process of law developed precisely to bar extralegal adjudications. Rather than merely set a standard for the courts, they evolved primarily to preclude any binding adjudication outside the courts.

Proper Clause says more than it does, it cannot authorize any administrative violation of an enumerated right. The Bill of Rights and other constitutionally enumerated rights are limits on the government's power, and thus even the most expansive power cannot justify administrative violations of constitutional rights. All the same, it will be seen that this has happened.

FEDERALISM. A further problem with federal administrative power is its interference with state law. Under the Constitution's Supremacy Clause, federal laws defeat state laws. But (as recognized by Bradford Clark) the clause specifies that only federal laws "made in pursuance" of the Constitution have this trumping effect. Thus, under the Constitution, although statutes enacted by Congress render contrary state laws void, mere agency rules and interpretations do not.

Nonetheless, agency rules and interpretations defeat state laws – including the states' constitutions, statutes, and common law – all on the theory that Congress authorized the agencies and that the agencies are merely specifying what Congress said in its enactments. The Constitution, however, reserves the trumping authority of federal law for acts of Congress, and thus not for the acts of agencies authorized by Congress. And in many instances – notably, when agencies interpret statutes – they are acting only under the authority of congressional ambiguity or silence, thus rendering any congressional authority utterly fictitious.

The effect is to deprive Americans of their freedom under the US Constitution to govern themselves through their elected state governments. Rather than enjoy self-government in layers of local and state elections, subject to the supremacy of federal laws, Americans now find that their state choices get crushed by unconstitutional assertions of the supremacy of administrative power.

* * *

By now it should be evident that the US Constitution systematically precludes administrative power. Extralegal governance is a type of absolute power, and regardless of whether it is called "prerogative" or "administrative," the Constitution bars it. In particular, the Constitution carefully authorizes the government to bind Americans and the states only through acts of Congress and the courts. It thereby forbids the government from evading these avenues of power by going down other pathways. Accordingly, when agencies issue binding rules or adjudications, or when they issue waivers, they are violating the Constitution.

The Constitution's Procedural Rights

The Supreme Court repudiates extralegal or absolute power not only with its structures but also with its guarantees of procedural rights. The administrative violation of these rights makes it especially clear that administrative power is a serious assault on civil liberties.

DUE PROCESS. The Fifth Amendment guarantees "the due process of law" and thereby bars the government from working outside the courts to issue orders to particular persons – whether to testify or even make an appearance. In defense of administrative adjudication, it often is suggested that due process is centrally a limit on the courts, not so much on the other parts of government.

As already evident, however, from the English history of due process, guarantees of due process of law developed precisely to bar extralegal adjudications. Rather than merely set a standard for the courts, they evolved primarily to preclude any binding adjudication outside the courts – a meaning summarized in the principle "None shall be put to answer without due process of law." This is why the English asserted the due process of law against the High Commission and the Star Chamber. And this is a large part of what the Fifth Amendment accomplished by guaranteeing due process.

The implication for adjudication outside the courts was recognized by one of the earliest academic commentators on the Bill of Rights. When lecturing on the Constitution at William & Mary, the Virginia judge St. George Tucker quoted the Fifth Amendment's Due Process Clause and concluded: "Due process of law must then be had before a judicial court, or a judicial magistrate." Similarly, Chancellor James Kent explained that the due process of law "means law, in its regular course of administration, through courts of law." And Justice Joseph Story echoed both Tucker and Kent. So much for administrative adjudication!

On behalf of the administrative evasion of due process, it may be said that due process has been expanded, and this has some truth. Ever since *Goldberg v. Kelly* in 1970 and *Mathews v. Eldridge* in 1976, there has been a due process right to a hearing before the government cuts off some welfare benefits, and the result has been to expand the availability of some process. This, however, is only part of the story.

Goldberg and *Mathews* offer only a smidgeon of administrative process for denials of some *benefits*, and are part of a broader jurisprudence that accepts a profound denial of due process for administrative *constraints*. There once was a constitutional right to the full due process of law in the courts of law for binding

adjudications – adjudications that impose legal obligation – whether in cutting off life or restricting liberty or
property. This essential right, however, has been reduced
to a mere administrative "hearing" (often where one cannot be heard) and more typically "something less."

The familiar result is that federal agencies can demand
testimony and private records and can impose fines without even going to court, let alone offering much administrative process. Most dramatically, the United States can
now simply detain some Americans without trial – as evident from *Hamdi v. Rumsfeld.* Yaser Esam Hamdi was a US
citizen who was captured as an enemy combatant, and as
he apparently remained a citizen, he traditionally would
have had a due process right to a trial in court with a jury
and the full due process of a criminal prosecution. But the
Supreme Court relied on *Mathews* to conclude that the
government owed Hamdi nothing more than an administrative decision about his status by a neutral adjudicator.

The sort of doctrine evident in *Goldberg* and *Mathews*
thus strains at a gnat and swallows the proverbial camel. It
secures negligible administrative process in some benefit
cases while accepting ruinous denials of due process in
constraint cases. The overall effect is to expand due process very marginally at the edges and to eviscerate the
right at its core.

JURY RIGHTS. Like due process, the right to a jury bars administrative and other extralegal adjudication. Juries are available only in the courts, and the right to a jury, in both civil and criminal cases, thus precludes binding adjudication in other tribunals.

Early Americans understood this. For example, in the decade after American independence, the legislatures of New Jersey and New Hampshire authorized judicial proceedings before justices of the peace – in the one state, qui tam forfeiture proceedings with a six-man jury, and in the other, small claims actions without a jury. Rather than accept these evasions of regular judicial proceedings, the courts of these states (New Jersey in 1780 and New Hampshire in 1786) held the statutes void for violating the right to a jury.

Although the US Constitution in 1789 guaranteed juries only in criminal cases, this prompted an outcry that juries also needed to be guaranteed in civil cases. The Seventh Amendment therefore secured the right to a jury in "Suits at common law." If, instead, the amendment had provided for juries "in common-law actions," it would have allowed the government to avoid juries in statutory actions. And if it had provided for juries "in existing common-law actions," it would have allowed the government to avoid juries in newly created actions. But the phrase "Suits at common law" meant civil suits brought in the common-law system, as opposed to those brought in equity or admiralty. Thus, in addition to the debates leading up to the Bill of Rights, the Seventh Amendment's very words make clear that the Amendment does not exclude statutory actions, least of all statutory actions in administrative proceedings. Instead, it secures juries in all civil cases other than those in equity and admiralty.

Nowadays, however, the Supreme Court says that the government's interest in congressionally authorized administrative adjudication trumps the right to a jury. In the Court's strange locution, where the government is acting administratively under newly created statutory "public rights," its public rights defeat the private assertion of the constitutional right to a jury trial.

The Court traditionally had used the term "public rights" merely as a label for the lawful spheres of executive action. In a series of cases, however – notably in 1977 in *Atlas Roofing v. Occupational Safety and Health Review Commission* – the Court unmoored the phrase from its traditional usage and used it to displace the Seventh Amendment right to a jury in civil cases. As it happens, binding agency adjudication, including fact-finding, is not within the scope of the Constitution's grant of executive power; even if it were, it would not defeat the Seventh Amendment, for the Constitution's rights are limits on government power. In other words, rights trump power. Understanding this obstacle, the Supreme Court in *Atlas Roofing* recast administrative power as a right – indeed, as a "public right." It thereby, in effect, denigrated the constitutional right to a jury as a mere private right and allowed the government's "public" right to defeat the private constitutional right.

This public-rights reasoning is a disgraceful assault on the Bill of Rights. On such reasoning, all rights are at risk.

Even where agencies are resolving disputes between merely private parties, the Supreme Court justifies the jury-less proceedings with the public-rights theory. The public right that eviscerates the Seventh Amendment is therefore not the government's legal claim in any particular administrative proceeding but merely the government's interest in administrative adjudication.

The Court thus sweepingly applies its generalization about "public rights" to all administrative adjudications, without pausing to consider whether the Constitution's right to a jury might, at least occasionally, prevail against the government's public rights. Administrative agencies can therefore, as a matter of course, violate the Constitution's jury rights without worrying about the strength of their claim of public rights.

OTHER PROCEDURAL RIGHTS. The antiadministrative implications of jury and due process rights are merely the beginning. In fact, almost all of the Constitution's procedural rights – including most provisions of the Bill of Rights – were designed not only to set standards in court but also to defeat extralegal adjudication.

Of course, different types of administrative proceedings violate different procedural guarantees. Where administrative adjudication is civil in nature, it evades the Constitution's procedures for civil cases; where it is criminal in nature, it evades the Constitution's procedures for criminal prosecutions.

Consider, for example, warrants for search and seizure. When the Fourth Amendment established its requirements for warrants, it was understood that a legally binding warrant for a search or seizure was an exercise of judicial power. Thus, both the Fourth Amendment and Article III (which grants judicial power to the courts) require a legally binding warrant to come from a judge or a justice of the peace. These provisions preclude administrative warrants.

Procedural rights have been transformed. No longer guarantees for the people, they now are merely options for the government.

Nonetheless, binding administrative warrants have become commonplace.

More broadly, the phrasing of almost all the procedural rights discloses that they bar administrative power. Rather than actively state that the courts cannot violate various procedures, the procedural rights are typically stated in the passive voice, and they thereby limit government in general, including Congress and the executive.

Also revealing is the placement of most procedural rights after the main body of the Constitution. To bar adjudication outside the courts, the procedural amendments could not simply modify Article III of the Constitution, for then they would have limited only the courts. They also had to limit the executive, established in Article II. They even had to limit Congress, established in Article I, lest Congress authorize adjudication outside the courts.

The drafters of the Bill of Rights therefore changed how they wrote it. They originally framed amendments that would have rewritten particular articles of the Constitution – altering their wording, article by article, section by section. Ultimately, however, the drafters added their amendments at the end of the whole Constitution. This was crucial, for it allowed the procedural amendments to limit all parts of government.

These two drafting techniques – the passive voice and amendments at the end – give the procedural rights their breadth. Had the drafters merely made adjustments to Article III, or otherwise focused exclusively on the courts, they would have left the barn door open for administrative evasions of procedural rights. With the passive voice and amendments at the end, however, the procedural rights make clear that they limit all parts of government. They thereby bar all binding adjudication outside the courts, including administrative adjudication.

Nonetheless, agencies impose binding adjudication outside the courts, without judges and juries. They issue summons, subpoenas, warrants, and fines without the due process of law of the courts. They deny equal discovery, as required by due process, where agency actions are civil in nature. And they impose prosecutorial discovery, which is forbidden by due process, in cases that are criminal in nature. They even reverse the burdens of proof and persuasion required by due process. Agencies thereby repeatedly deprive Americans of their procedural rights.

REDUCTION OF CONSTITUTIONAL GUARANTEES TO MERE OPTIONS. The seriousness of the administrative evasion of procedural rights has not been sufficiently recognized. It becomes apparent, however, when one realizes that the government now enjoys ambidextrous enforcement.

The government once could engage in binding adjudication against Americans only through the courts and their judges. Now, it can choose administrative adjudication. In some instances, Congress alone makes this choice; in others, it authorizes an agency, such as the SEC, to make the selection. One way or another, the government can act ambidextrously – either through the courts and their judges, juries, and due process or through administrative adjudication and its faux process.

The evasion thereby changes the very nature of procedural rights. Such rights traditionally were assurances against the government. Now they are but one of the choices for government in its exercise of power. Though the government must respect these rights when it proceeds against Americans in court, it has the freedom to escape them by taking an administrative path. Procedural rights have thereby been transformed. No longer guarantees for the people, they now are merely options for the government.

SUBSTANTIVE RIGHTS. The administrative evasion of procedural rights is especially worrisome because it facilitates violations of substantive rights. Although this is a danger for many such rights, including religious liberty and assembling to petition, the threat is clearest for the freedoms of speech and the press, as they traditionally were understood in procedural terms.

The central historical understanding of speech and press rights was as a freedom from licensing – from the requirement of having to get prior administrative permission. And when such rights were threatened by postpublication prosecutions, they were recognized to be dependent on the right to a jury trial.

It therefore is shocking that the federal government uses administrative proceedings, including administrative licensing, to regulate words and speakers. The Federal Election Commission regulates political participation, and to avoid the fines it imposes through administrative adjudication, political speakers often ask the commission for advisory opinions – thus enabling the commission to license their political speech. The Federal Communications Commission imposes administrative licensing on broadcasters and thereby limits what they say. The SEC uses this sort of licensing to regulate some financial disclosures. Least well known but perhaps most dangerous, Health and Human Services establishes licensing, conducted by institutional review boards, for what is said in much empirical academic research and even for what can be published about it. (This last type of licensing is especially egregious because it limits the production and publication of medical knowledge. In thus limiting the ability of doctors to save lives, Institutional Review Boards leave a body count larger than that of Vietnam.) To be sure, the government needs to regulate some of the things it licenses; most clearly, it needs to allocate airwaves among broadcasters. But this does not mean it needs to regulate through administrative proceedings, let alone the prior administrative licensing of words.

The underlying constitutional danger is a wholesale mode of control. Traditionally, the government could engage in only retail suppression. It had to prove its case before a judge and jury in the course of prosecuting a particular person for his particular words. Nowadays, the government can employ administrative proceedings against words and even speakers, thereby avoiding the difficulty of persuading judges and juries. And by using licensing against speech or speakers – that is, by forcing potential speakers to seek prior administrative permission – the government can go further than is usual even in most administrative proceedings in reversing the usual burdens of proof and persuasion. The administrative evasion of procedural rights thus enables the government to avoid the difficulties of retail prosecutions. Indeed, it allows the government to engage in the sort of wholesale control of words and speakers that, unsurprisingly, last flourished in common-law nations in the seventeenth century.

*　*　*

Reflecting their origins as obstacles to extralegal pathways, the Constitution's procedural rights preclude administrative adjudication. Not merely the Constitution's structures but even its procedural rights bar administrative power. Administrative power, however, ignores all of this. It even reduces procedural rights to mere options for government, and reintroduces prior licensing and its wholesale control of speech. It is difficult to think of a more serious civil liberties problem for the twenty-first century.

Procedural Deprivations in Court

Sadly, the loss of procedural rights in administrative tribunals is not the end of the matter. When hearing appeals from administrative adjudications, judges protect these proceedings in ways that further violate of procedural rights. The result is a double violation of rights, initially by agencies and then by the courts themselves.

JUDICIAL BIAS IN DEFERENCE TO AGENCY INTERPRETATION. When agencies make law in the guise of interpreting statutes, they rely on the courts to defer to their interpretations. But this judicial deference is unconstitutional.

One problem is the judicial abandonment of independent judgment. When judges defer to agency interpretations, they depart from their judicial office or duty, under Article III of the Constitution, to exercise their own independent judgment. Recognizing this duty, Chief Justice John Marshall wrote in *Marbury v. Madison*: "It is emphatically the province and duty of the judicial department to say what the law is. Those who apply the rule to particular cases, must of necessity expound and interpret that rule." The judges therefore cannot defer to an agency's interpretation without abandoning their duty – indeed, their very office – as judges.

But this is not all; it gets worse. When the government is a party to a case, the doctrines that require judicial deference to agency interpretation are precommitments in favor of the government's legal position, and the effect is systematic judicial bias. Of course, this is an institutional rather than a personal predisposition, but it is therefore all the more systematic in favoring the most powerful of parties. One might object that the judges are said to defer in other areas of law. Such other "deference," however, is usually little more than deference to the law itself and its allocation of power. It never is deference to a single party. The

doctrines that require judicial deference to agency interpretation thus stand out as dangerous violations of the
Fifth Amendment's due process of law.

Put bluntly, what ordinarily is called "*Chevron* deference"
(to agency interpretations of statutes) is really *Chevron*
bias. Similarly, "*Auer* deference" (to agency interpretations
of rules, often in the form of guidance) is really *Auer* bias.
And although "*Mead-Skidmore* respect" (for informal
agency interpretation of statutes) is not as predictable, it
also is a form of bias. All such deference grossly violates
the most basic due process right to be judged without any
judicial precommitment to the other party.

Incidentally, the judges do not need to use any such
deference. They sometimes say they need to rely on agency
interpretation to fill statutory gaps because they otherwise
would have to create law in such spaces. But judges should
neither make law nor defer to agency interpretations. If,
after the judges apply their usual tools of interpretation,
they can find no further meaning in a statute, they should
simply declare that the ambiguous provision has no discern-
able meaning – thereby leaving the ambiguity to be cured by
Congress. The judges therefore do not need to defer to the
government's legal position. The bias is unnecessary.

Just how severe is the bias problem? The first canon of

judicial conduct declares: "An independent and honorable judiciary is indispensable to justice in our society." And the third canon states that a judge "shall disqualify himself or herself in a proceeding in which the judge's impartiality might reasonably be questioned, including but not limited to instances in which . . . the judge has a personal bias or prejudice concerning a party." The implications are sobering because the institutional bias that comes with judicial deference is much more systematic and far reaching than any personal bias.

DEFERENCE TO AGENCY FACT-FINDING: LOST JURY RIGHTS AND JUDICIAL BIAS. When a court reviews an agency adjudication, the judges rely on the agency's fact-finding, as preserved in its administrative record. And this deprives parties of both jury and due process rights.

When a court defers to agency fact-finding, it deprives Americans of their right to a jury trial. As it happens, juries (like other procedural rights) are a constitutional right in the first instance; not merely later when one gets to court – a point decided in some of the earliest American constitutional cases. But even after one appeals from an agency to a court, one still does not get a jury trial. The excuse is that an agency's administrative record is like the record of a lower court. But an agency record is not the record of a court, let alone the verdict of a jury. When a court relies on such a record, the court itself violates jury rights.

Even worse is the bias. Where the government is a party to a case, the judges are relying on a record that is merely one party's version of the facts. Accordingly, when thus deferring to the administrative record, the judges are favoring one of the parties. Judicial deference to the administrative record is therefore another type of systematic bias, in violation of the Fifth Amendment's due process of law.

In court cases, there are two types of questions, those of law and those of fact. The combination of the two types of deference – to an agency's interpretation and to its record – is therefore especially disturbing. It means that, where the government is a party, there is systematic judicial bias in favor of the government on both the law and the facts. What, then, is left for the unbiased judgment of a judge and jury?

JUDICIAL BIAS EVEN AFTER HOLDING AGENCY ACTS UNLAWFUL. Even after courts hold agency actions unlawful, they continue to deny due process rights. For example, they usually will hesitate to declare an unlawful agency action void – instead remanding it to the agency. More-over, when a district or circuit court interprets an ambiguous statute administered by an agency, the Supreme Court, under the *Brand X* doctrine, allows the agency in subsequent matters to disregard the judicial precedent and follow its own interpretation – thereby denying Americans the ability to secure precedent through litigation.

*   *   *

The courts should condemn the extralegal adjudication conducted by agencies, not least because it guts procedural rights. Instead, the courts add their own assaults on procedural rights. The result is the double violation of such rights, both administrative and judicial.

Jurisdictional Boundaries

Although the US Constitution generally repudiates extralegal power, there are some interesting qualifications at the edges. What are these limits to the argument? They tend to involve jurisdictional boundaries.

The preeminent jurisdictional qualification concerns the states. The states have varying constitutions, and although most of them establish principles very similar to those of the US Constitution, some have clearly gone in other directions – as when Virginia amended its constitution in 1971 to authorize administrative power. A state that goes too far in this direction may be vulnerable under the US Constitution's guarantee of a republican form of government. Up to that point, however, the Constitution does not prevent the states from taking their own paths.

Another jurisdictional caveat is local. When the English developed constitutional ideals against extralegal power, they largely succeeded in defeating the king's centralized prerogative power, but they typically did not think their ideals were applicable to local and other noncentralized extralegal power – what nowadays would be considered localized administrative power. This localized administrative power – such as the power exercised by justices of the peace, commissioners of sewers, and bankruptcy commissioners – was in tension with English constitutional ideals, but the English generally did not pursue such ideals at the local level.

And this pattern has been repeated in America. Although many state constitutions embrace ideals that preclude extralegal power, such constitutions have often been understood to permit some local administrative power. Moreover, where Congress acts in place of the states (in the territories and the District of Columbia), it has always felt free to authorize at least some local administrative measures, such as licensing regulations and non–Article III judges.

Another jurisdictional limit is at the borders. Congress

for a long time (until the early twentieth century) understood that it could not nationally authorize the executive to regulate through licensing in domestic matters. Nonetheless, the US Constitution has always been understood to allow Congress to authorize licensing regulation in cross-border matters – traditionally Indian traders and steamboats and now, for example, airplanes and pilots.

Yet another jurisdictional boundary arises from military law. As recognized by the Constitution, the military has always been subject to its own legal system, in which military law and adjudication can be delegated.

Finally, it should be recalled that the argument here against administrative power is confined to edicts that bind or unbind. The Constitution does not bar the executive from

When the government is a party to a case, the doctrines that require judicial deference to agency interpretation are precommitments in favor of the government's legal position, and the effect is systematic judicial bias.

making rules and establishing adjudication for the direction of its officers, for the distribution of benefits, or for determining the status of immigrants.

These jurisdictional qualifications are not merely exceptions but valuable boundaries to the Constitution's principles. By leaving room for administrative power in the states, in localities, at the borders, and so forth, these limits allow Americans to establish strong principles against extralegal power in the US Constitution. In other words, the federal barriers against extralegal power could be so unequivocal precisely because they did not reach too far – because they did not extend beyond the national regulation of domestic matters.

The German Connection

If the Constitution bars administrative power, how did this power enter American law? And why does it look so much like the old absolute power?

The answer lies in the civil law – the academic study of Roman law – which often celebrated Roman-style imperial power. On this foundation, Continental civilians justified their notions of absolute power, and English kings and their civilian-trained advisors introduced such ideas into England.

The ensuing tension between English law and civilian absolutist ideas has shaped the development of constitutional law. The English in the seventeenth century developed constitutional ideals in opposition to absolute power, and Americans took such ideals even further in the US Constitution. But Continental peoples were not so fortunate. Their rulers and sympathetic academics, not least in Germany, tended to celebrate absolutism, and on this basis often defeated claims for constitutions, for separation of powers, and for bills of rights.

Especially in Prussia and other German states, rulers and attendant academics developed the monarch's personal absolute power into the state's bureaucratic administrative power. The Prussians were leaders in this development in the seventeenth and eighteenth centuries, and were echoed by the Russians in the 1760s and the French beginning in the 1790s. By the nineteenth century, the Prussians were considered the preeminent theorists and practitioners of administrative power.

This survival of absolute power in administrative form had consequences beyond the Continent. From there, notably Germany, absolute power in administrative form circled back to the common-law countries. The English turned to Continental administrative ideas already in the mid-nineteenth century, and Americans did so shortly afterward. Thousands of nineteenth-century Americans traveled to study in German universities, and when they returned home, they brought back ideas of administrative power. Some of them even spread their Germanic notions in Asia – as when Frank Goodnow drafted the 1914 Chinese Constitution.

The American adoption of European administrative ideas reveals that it is an understatement to say that federal administrative power revives absolute power. In fact, federal administrative power is a direct continuation of the absolutism that persisted in administrative form on the Continent.

This derivation of administrative power from Continental and especially German ideas is not only explanatory but also worrisome. In Europe, such ideas justified absolute power even within largely elected governments and, more broadly, undermined the expectation of free peoples that they could govern themselves, whether politically or even personally. Commenting on how Germans were coming to feel dependent on order imposed from above, Max Weber called them "Ordnungsmenschen."

Similarly, in this country, Americans are becoming accustomed to being ruled. This was Tocqueville's fear, and increasingly it is a reality. The danger is not merely a loss of civil liberties but a loss of the independent and self-governing spirit upon which all civil liberties depend.

Administrative Power and Equal Voting Rights

To understand how profoundly administrative governance threatens civil liberties, consider the growth of equal suffrage and the expansion of administrative power. Voting rights and the administrative state have probably been the two most remarkable developments in the federal government since the Civil War. It therefore is worth pausing to ask whether there is a connection.

Federal law was slow to protect equal suffrage. In 1870, the Fifteenth Amendment gave blacks the right to vote. In 1920, women acquired this right. And in 1965, the equality for blacks began to become a widespread reality.

Administrative power tended to expand in the wake of these changes in suffrage (a curiosity first noted by Thomas West). In 1887, Congress established the first major federal administrative agency, the Interstate Commerce Commission. In the 1930s, the New Deal created a host of powerful new agencies. And since the 1960s, federal administrative power has expanded even further. Of course, it would be a mistake to link administrative power too narrowly to the key dates in the expansion of suffrage. But growing popular participation in representative politics has evidently been accompanied by a shift of legislative power out of Congress and into administrative agencies.

The explanation is not hard to find. Although equality in voting rights has been widely accepted, the resulting democratization of American politics has prompted misgivings. Worried about the rough-and-tumble character of representative politics, and about the tendency of newly enfranchised groups to reject progressive reforms, many Americans have sought what they consider a more elevated mode of governance.

Some early progressives were quite candid about this. Woodrow Wilson complained that "the reformer is bewildered" by the need to persuade "a voting majority of several million heads." He was particularly worried about the diversity of the nation, which meant that the reformer needed to influence "the mind, not of Americans of the older stocks only, but also of Irishmen, of Germans, of Negroes." Elaborating this point, he observed: "The bulk of mankind is rigidly unphilosophical, and nowadays the bulk of mankind votes." And "where is this unphilosophical bulk of mankind more multifarious in its composition than in the United States?" Accordingly, "in order to get a footing for new doctrine, one must influence minds cast in every mold of race, minds inheriting every bias of environment, warped by the histories of a score of different nations, warmed or chilled, closed or expanded by almost every climate of the globe." Rather than try to persuade such persons, Wilson welcomed administrative governance. The people could still have their republic, but much legislative power would be shifted out of an elected body and into the hands of the right sort of people.

Rather than narrowly a matter of racism, this has been a transfer of legislative power to the knowledge class – meaning not a class defined in Marxist or other economic terms but those persons whose identity or sense of self-worth centers on their knowledge. More than merely the intelligentsia, this class includes all who are more attached to the authority of knowledge than to the authority of local political communities. Which is not to say that they have been particularly knowledgeable, but that their sense of affinity with cosmopolitan knowledge, rather than local connectedness, has been the foundation of their influence and identity. And in appreciating the authority they have attributed to their knowledge, and distrusting the tumultuous politics of a diverse people, they have gradually moved legislative power out of Congress and into administrative agencies – to be exercised, in more genteel ways, by persons like . . . themselves.

The enfranchised masses, in short, have disappointed those who think they know better. Walter Lippmann worried that "what thwarts the growth of our civilization is . . . the faltering method, the distracted soul, and the murky

vision of what we grandiloquently call the will of the people."
More recently, Peter Orszag urges that "bold measures are
needed to circumvent polarization" – in particular that
America needs to overcome the resulting "gridlock of our
political institutions by making them a bit less democratic."

Of course, the removal of legislative power from the
representatives of a diverse people has implications for
minorities. Leaving aside Wilson's overt racism, the problem is the relocation of lawmaking power a further step
away from the people and into the hands of a relatively
homogenized class. Even when exercised with solicitude
for minorities, it is a sort of power exercised from above,
and those who dominate the administrative state have
always been if not white men, then at least members of
the knowledge class.

It therefore should be no surprise that administrative
power comes with costs for the classes and attachments
that are more apt to find expression through representative
government. In contrast to the power exercised by elected
members of Congress, administrative power comes with
little accountability to – or even sympathy for – local,
regional, religious, and other distinctive communities.
Individually, administrators may be concerned about all
Americans, but their power is structured in a way designed
to cut off the political demands with which, in a

representative system of government, local and other distinctive communities can protect themselves.

Administrative power thus cannot be understood apart from equal voting rights. The gain in popular suffrage has been accompanied by disdain for the choices made through a representative system and a corresponding shift of legislative power out of Congress. Although the redistribution of legislative power has gratified the knowledge class, it makes a mockery of the struggle for equal voting rights and confirms how severely administrative power threatens civil liberties.

Is It Practicable to Abandon Administrative Power?

Although administrative power is the nation's preeminent threat to civil liberties, many commentators worry that the nation cannot get along without it. In fact, the resulting economic problems suggest that the nation cannot afford to retain administrative power. But even so, it remains to be considered whether government is practicable without it.

For example, is administrative power the only means of rapid legislative change? Actually, when Congress wishes, it can act faster than most agencies, while relying on their expertise. Popular complaints about congressional "gridlock" therefore do not usually reflect the realities of institutional impediments, but instead typically serve to justify circumventing the political obstacles inherent in representative government.

Let's pretend, however, that gridlock is an institutional rather than a political impediment. How much administrative power actually involves genuine emergencies – matters that simply cannot wait for Congress to act? In fact, most administrative power effectuates long-term policies, and most claims of emergencies are merely excuses to shift power out of Congress.

Does complexity require administrative power? Federal statutes obviously can be just as complex as agency rules. The only difference is that statutes are adopted by Congress rather than by agencies. Of course, the underlying question (asked by Richard Epstein) is whether our complex society really needs complex rules, and there is reason to fear that the administrative answer to this is deeply mistaken.

Even if rules were adopted by Congress rather than agencies, how would the courts be able to handle the vast amount of adjudication currently handled by agencies? Apologists for administrative power protest that there are over ten thousand administrative adjudicators whose work could not be handled by the courts. But the vast bulk of such adjudication does not impose legal obligation. Thus, rather than administrative power, most such adjudication is merely the ordinary and lawful exercise of executive power – for example, in determining the distribution of benefits or the status of immigrants.

Accordingly, the question as to whether courts could handle what is now administrative adjudication must focus on the agency adjudication that imposes legal obligation. For example, the SEC employs only 5 administrative law judges, the Occupational Safety and Health Review Commission has 12, and the National Labor Relations Board has 34. In fact, outside the Social Security Administration, which distributes benefits, there are only 257 administrative law judges. This is not an overwhelming number, and it suggests that the scale of administrative adjudication is grossly overstated. The work of at least these 257 administrative law judges could easily be handled with the addition of an equivalent number of real judges.

What about the value of impartial administrative expertise? It is not clear that agencies have greater expertise than the private sector. Indeed, industry has much influence over agency regulation in part because of industry's greater knowledge. Some agencies are so short of expertise that they rely on regulated industries to write the regulations – as happened, for example, with the 2010 net neutrality rules.

More generally, expert knowledge must be distinguished from expert decision making. A decision to adopt a regulation in one area of expertise will almost inevitably have consequences in other fields of knowledge, and expertise in the one area is therefore not enough to resolve whether the regulation should be adopted. Indeed, a person with specialized expertise will tend to overestimate the importance of that area and underestimate the significance of others. As a result, although experts can be valuable for

In appreciating the authority they have attributed to their knowledge, and distrusting the tumultuous politics of a diverse people, the knowledge class has gradually moved legislative power out of Congress and into administrative agencies—to be exercised by persons like themselves.

their specialized knowledge, they usually cannot be relied upon for decisions that take a balanced view of the consequences. This is why administrative power so frequently seems harsh or disproportionate: the administrative experts focus so closely on what they care about that they fail adequately to see other aspects of the question. It therefore makes sense to get the views of experts, but not to rely on them for decisions about regulation.

Ultimately, the question as to whether the government can get along without administrative power should be answered by its proponents. The arguments about the need for administrative power are empirical, and those who assert the need to depart from the Constitution must bear the burden of proof. Nonetheless, the advocates of administrative power rarely, if ever, back up their claims with serious empirical evidence.

Meanwhile, the empirical evidence of the danger from administrative power is mounting. Not being directly accountable to the people – or even to judges who act without bias – administrative power crushes the life and livelihood out of entire classes of Americans, depriving them of work and even of lifesaving medicines. It therefore is difficult to avoid the conclusion that, overall, the administrative assault on basic freedoms is unnecessary and even dangerous.

What Is To Be Done?

Lenin asked his fellow Russians, "What is to be done?" Fortunately for Americans, the answer is not revolution but a traditional American defense of civil liberties.

To this end, Americans will have to work through all three branches of government. Of course, none of the branches has thus far revealed much capacity to limit administrative power. But this is all the more reason to consider what they can do before it is too late.

First, although Congress has repeatedly authorized and acquiesced in administrative power, it still perhaps can redeem itself. Most basically, Congress should reclaim its legislative power. And, of course, it need not do this all at once; instead, it can convert rules to statutes at a measured pace, agency by agency. By leaving so much lawmaking to the executive, our legislators have allowed not only power but also leadership and even fundraising to shift to the president. Ambitious legislators might therefore realize the advantages of reclaiming their constitutional role.

Congress also should bar judicial deference to agencies on questions of law or fact, as this violates due process and other constitutional limitations. Congress additionally should abolish administrative law judges and replace them with real judges (a reform it can partly fund by shifting money from the unconstitutional adjudicators to the courts). More generally, Congress should remove immunity for administrators – beginning with those who have desk jobs in agencies with a track record of violating constitutional rights.

The executive offers a second mechanism against administrative power. Presidents come and go, and a president worried about administrative power should not be content merely to put bad administrative policies on hold until the next election; more seriously, he should end administrative paths of governance. For example, he could require agencies, one by one, to send their rules to Congress for it to adopt. He also could require federal lawyers to refrain from seeking judicial deference, lest they participate in the courts' due process violations. For any president, such steps would be a remarkable constitutional legacy.

A third and more predictable approach will be through the courts. The judges have repeatedly acquiesced in administrative power. Between 1906 and 1912 and again in 1937, the judges who stood up against it were threatened, and each time they gave way. Subsequently, even without threats, the judges have bent over backward to accommodate such power.

They thereby have corrupted their own proceedings – for example, by refusing jury rights even in court, by abandoning their office of independent judgment, and by engaging in systematic bias in violation of the due process of law. Overall, administrative power is one of the most shameful episodes in the history of the federal judiciary.

Nonetheless, Americans can persuade the judges to do their duty. The judges have high ideals of their office of independent judgment. And they are dedicated to their role in upholding the law, especially the Constitution. Accordingly, once they understand how administrative power corrupts the processes of the courts and violates constitutional liberties, at least some of them will repudiate it.

Ultimately, the defeat of administrative power will have to come from the people. Only their spirit of liberty can move Congress, inspire the president, and brace the judges to do their duty.

Americans therefore need to recognize that administrative power revives absolute power and profoundly threatens civil liberties. Once Americans understand this, they can begin to push back, and the fate of administrative power will then be only a matter of time.

Portions of this book were originally published in *City Journal* and RealClearPolicy.com.

First American edition published in 2017 by Encounter Books, an activity of Encounter for Culture and Education, Inc., a nonprofit, tax exempt corporation.
Encounter Books website address: www.encounterbooks.com

Manufactured in the United States and printed on acid-free paper. The paper used in this publication meets the minimum requirements of ANSI/NISO Z39.48–1992 (R 1997) (*Permanence of Paper*).

FIRST AMERICAN EDITION

LIBRARY OF CONGRESS CATALOGING-IN-PUBLICATION DATA

Names: Hamburger, Philip, 1957– author.
Title: The administrative threat / by Philip Hamburger.
Description: New York : Encounter Books, 2017. | Series: Encounter intelligence ; 3
Identifiers: LCCN 2017001972 (print) | LCCN 2017006942 (ebook) | ISBN 9781594039492 (pbk. : alk. paper) | ISBN 9781594039508 (Ebook)
Subjects: LCSH: Abuse of administrative power—United States.
Classification: LCC KF5423 .H36 2017 (print) | LCC KF5423 (ebook) | DDC 342.73/06—dc23
LC record available at https://lccn.loc.gov/2017001972

10 9 8 7 6 5 4 3 2 1